Let Me Walk The Journey With You

Healing Through The Chakras

A collection of stories, poems, and reflections by women on the journey with cancer

Powerful You!
PUBLISHING
Sharing Wisdom ~ Shining Light

Let Me Walk The Journey With You
Healing Through The Chakras

Copyright © 2015

Published by: Powerful You! Inc. USA
www.powerfulyoupublishing.com

Library of Congress Control Number: 2015958253

ISBN: 9780997066104

First Edition December 2015

Body, Mind & Spirit: Healing - Energy

Printed in the United States of America

DEDICATION

This book is dedicated to every woman battling cancer on their journey to healing. May you find hope, courage, and connection in these stories.

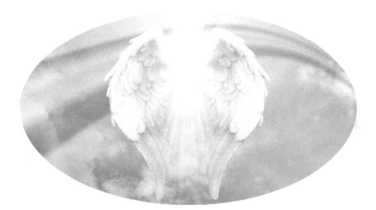

Table of Contents

"We are each of us Angels with one wing,
and we can only fly by embracing each other."
~ Luciano de Crescenzo

FOREWORD
Journey

Sister Carol A. Jaruszewski R.S.M.

Let me walk the journey with you
Is this a statement, question, or invitation?

Let me walk the journey with you
Who speaks these words to you?
Your doctor, nurse, another patient, child, sibling, friend,
your spouse, your God, a Higher Power, or Divine Spirit

Let me walk the journey with you through the dark,
leading to the energy and beauty of red roses, orange
daylilies, yellow daffodils, green clover, teal oceans, pink
sunsets, blue skies, indigo nights, purple violets into the
snowdrops of the daylight.

Let me walk the journey with you
Will you hope, honor, imagine, laugh, learn, listen, love,
read, relax, and revere?

Let me walk the journey with you
Will you embrace, empathize, empower, encourage,
initiate, inspire, respect, tease, thank, and touch?

Let me walk the journey with you accompanying,
affirming, caring, consoling, creating, pondering, praying,
waiting, wondering, and dancing day by day.

Let us walk the journey together.

All is light and life, giving energy for the journey.

**It is all about the journey, living in the light of
mystery.**

INTRODUCTION
The Energy of Healing

Lynn Ferrer

There are many body maps found in *Gray's Anatomy* that describe the physical body, and beyond the physical systems lies a network of seven primary energy centers known as the Chakras. This energy anatomy plays a conscious role in our well-being. It is just as important, if not more important, than the physical. These centers record and store information about our experiences, beliefs, and values. Each chakra manages a specific area of information. We experience ourselves through the seven primary energy centers, and we also heal through them. This is a primary principal of Holistic Energy Healing, and this is exactly the work I do with my patients at Saint Barnabas Out-Patient Cancer Center.

By assessing the patient's energy system, I am able to determine, which Chakras are open and which are closed or leaking energy. Energy may be blocked not only due to physical reasons, but also for spiritual, emotional, and mental reasons. Through the use of holistic modalities such as Reiki, Reflexology, Guided Imagery and Meditation, just to name a few, I am able to teach and assist our patients to bring balance and harmony back into their lives.

We all have a story to tell, and this book shares the lives of nine courageous women battling cancer—their strength and challenges, their vulnerability and triumphs—as they live each day to its fullest. It is also a "love story" in the true sense of the word. It is a love of self, a love of one another, and then moving that love out into the community of women who on a daily basis balance cancer with their busy lives. This is accomplished through our organization called WINGS—Women Inspiring, Nurturing, Giving Strength and Support to other women with cancer. Please join us on our journey.

THE ENERGY CENTERS
The Chakras

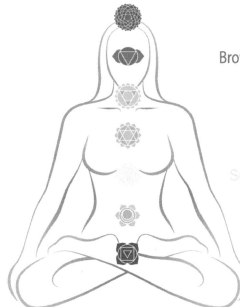

Crown Chakra

Brow/Third Eye Chakra

Throat Chakra

Heart Chakra

Solar Plexus Chakra

Sacral Chakra

Root Chakra

PROLOGUE
The Story Begins

Lynn Ferrer

"Once upon a time" is the classic beginning of most fairy tales: however this is not a fairy tale, but a true life story. It is the tale of two friends, a cruel twist of fate and a miracle. It is the legend of the caterpillar emerging as a butterfly, only after it has struggled through the dark cocoon.

Each of us may have experienced a similar situation in our own lives, and hopefully we have moved from the fear and shadow of the cocoon to the beauty and freedom of the butterfly in flight.

Our paths first crossed when I accepted the position of Infection Control Practitioner for Saint Barnabas Medical Center. While making rounds one day, I met Nancy on the telemetry unit. I remember thinking that this pretty young lady was probably about the same age as my own daughters. Once I moved into the position of Director of Infection Control & The HIV Program, I only saw Nan at occasional meetings. She had now moved up to the position of head nurse of the telemetry unit. She was young for this position, and she was handling it well.

My involvement with the HIV program expanded as the AIDS epidemic exploded. Besides the everyday work, we ran support groups for the HIV+ patients and also for their families. It was because of this agenda that I decided to earn a master's in counseling and became certified as a Holistic Nurse Practitioner. Both the patients and their loved ones had numerous emotional problems to deal with as well as the devastating disease itself.

In the meantime, Nan continued to advance in her career. When the Vice President of Nursing resigned, Nan was temporarily moved into her position and within months she was named the new VP. It didn't take long before she was promoted again to Senior Vice President of Patient Care Services for the entire system.

In the Spring of 2000, I heard a rumor that Nancy had undergone surgery for breast cancer and was about to start chemotherapy. I made some calls to confirm the rumor and found out that it was true. I was devastated! How could this happen to someone so beautiful and vibrant? Since I was now certified in Holistic Nursing, I called Nan's secretary who I knew and volunteered my services. Michelle informed me that Nan was hard to reach these days. I prayed for guidance and went on with my life.

As fate would have it, I was scheduled for a mammography at the Ambulatory Care Center the following week. Approaching the building, I noticed a couple standing in front apparently waiting for valet service. Upon closer observation, I realized it was Nan and her husband. I quickly pulled over, jumped out of my car and headed in their direction. The parking attendant was yelling, "Lady, you can't park over there." I paid no attention and hurried on my way. I put my arms around Nancy and looking into her eyes I whispered, "Nan let me walk the journey with you." She nodded and we made a date right then and there.

Our First Encounter

I was nervous about our first session. I wanted it to go perfectly. I checked and re-checked the bag I had packed earlier. It contained a small CD player and my favorite CD, *Reiki Hands of Light*, along with additional CDs, incense, a crystal pendulum, and lavender hand and body lotion. There was also a folder of handouts containing information on the Chakras, Reiki, Reflexology and Guided Imagery. I looked at my watch and decided it was time to go.

I arrived a few minutes early and did some deep breathing as I sat in my car. I turned the air conditioner up to high. My mind was buzzing with endless thoughts. What made me think I was a healer or could make a difference in her diagnosis? What kind of expert healing had I done so far? She deserved the very best and there were more experienced people out there. Face it, my biggest attribute was that I cared about Nancy and wanted to help her bring balance and healing back into her life. If that was the recipe, we were home free.

Anxiously, I got out of the car and walked up the path to the front door. I pressed the bell and almost instantly Nan opened the door and asked me in. I followed her downstairs to the playroom, where both of her children were watching TV. They turned immediately to see who was parading after their mom. You could easily tell by looking into their young eyes that things had been different around here lately. The fun and playfulness were glazed over by a film of fear. I sat down on the couch next to Nan and she explained that Bill hadn't come home from work yet, so the kids would be with us.

No sooner had I pulled the papers out of the bag, as if on cue, the kids were on top of Nancy. Since she had already introduced me, she informed them that I would be helping Mommy because she wasn't feeling good. Kaley immediate asked, "Are you going back to the hospital?" "I hope not," was Nan's reply.

I began talking about the energy systems of the body and the role they played in health and illness. Bored by the conversation, Kaley and Jon began jumping from chair to chair, sometimes missing and toppling to the floor. This was upsetting for Nan as she tried to get them to stop and watch their show. Just as I was thinking it was hopeless, Bill came home. The troops ran to meet their dad, and Nan asked that he keep them upstairs for a while so we could work. He agreed, but within minutes Kaley was at the top of the stairs crying and returned to us. Nan told her she could stay, but that she had to be quiet. She dutifully nodded her pretty head.

I decided to use headphones for Nan to keep the distractions to a minimum. I played a meditation CD by Dr. Brian Weiss, which is excellent for inducing relaxation. Moving down to the end of the sofa, I began doing reflexology. I could feel Nan begin to relax. Every so often Kaley would come over and touch her and talk to her, but Nan was able to go back to relaxing once she stopped.

By the end of the session I felt drained; however, Nan seemed to feel better. Saying goodbye at her front door, I offered to do the sessions at my house. Nan agreed that it was a much better solution since I did not have any small children. We made a date for the following week.

Nan began coming to my house for weekly sessions. We usually began by talking and sharing some of the important events that took place since our last session. She kept me updated on her medications and on the holistic modalities she was adding to her regimen.

We both did extensive reading on the subject and discussed the importance of keeping her stress level as low as possible. The fact that she had a husband and two small children would be enough to stress out anyone. On top of that, Nan was juggling a responsible position at the top of the corporate ladder.

As I sat across from her this particular evening, I felt that something new was on her mind. I placed my hands on her shoulders, looked directly into her eyes, and asked,

"What's happening? Why are you so sad?"

"I start chemo next week," she replied. "I don't think I'll be well enough to come here for our sessions."

I hugged her and whispered, "That's not a problem. I will come to chemo with you."

"That's impossible', she cried. "You have to work, and the time and dates are constantly changing."

I smiled and replied, "You have enough to worry about; let me handle this one." And so we began.

If you can say that there is anything good about a chemotherapy suite, then I must say that having individual rooms is a definite plus. The rooms are a fair size and contain a recliner, a couple of chairs, a rolling stool, a TV with a DVD player, and a boom box.

The usual procedure involved the nurse coming and doing baseline vital signs, then setting the I.V. and connecting the chemo. Nan was usually uptight at the beginning of each session, however once the chemo was running and things were on their way, we would begin a relaxation exercise. Together in the room, a certain peace filled this space, and fear was replaced by our spiritual connection.

A Tale of Two Spirits

I look out through the rain-spattered window on this dark and dreary night for signs of an approaching vehicle. All that's present are the raindrops splashing against the windowpane and the bleak, starless night. Nan is late for her appointment. I walk back to my chair, pick up my book and begin reading again. It's difficult to concentrate. My mind keeps wandering back to Nan's situation. It's so hard for her to come for an evening session because she has to leave her children after working all day, yet I know how good she feels after we finish. It benefits not only her body, but her mind and spirit are renewed as well.

I hear the sound of my bell. Thank God she's here. I open the door and am greeted by a frazzled Nan and her 3-year-old daughter Kaley. I can see the distress in Nan's eyes and hear it in her voice. I welcome them in as Nan is speaking. "She didn't want me to leave her tonight, Lynn. I know we won't be able to work, but I wanted to come over in person to explain it to you." "Let's just see what we can do," I responded as I took their jackets.

My family room was all set up. The reflexology chair was open in front of the fireplace. The essential oils and lotions were on a table next to the chair, along with the scented candles. By the head of the recliner, you could hear the water in the fountain dancing gently over the rocks.

I suggested to Nan that she sit in the chair with Kaley. I would place them in a relaxing position as I explained to Kaley what I was about to do with her mom. I then asked Kaley's permission and she nodded her head in consent. As she was getting herself comfortable resting on her mom, I lowered the lights and turned on soft, relaxing music.

I gently covered mother and daughter and positioned myself at the foot of the chair. I began our usual routine, a reflexology treatment in conjunction with a guided imagery. Both settled down quickly and appeared very relaxed. In a few minutes, their breathing slowed and became rhythmic. I was able to continue the treatment for a full hour.

In the final phase, I moved around the chair performing Reiki, the laying-on of hands to bring about relaxation, healing, and peace. I could genuinely feel the energy of both mother and child flowing freely. What a beautiful feeling and a welcoming gift. Watching the silhouette of this mother and child by the flickering flames was a most memorable and touching picture that has been etched in my heart forever.

Graduation

Nan continued to return to chemotherapy approximately every two weeks for several months. If her blood counts were low, it might be changed to a three-week span. I arranged my work schedule so that I could be with her each time. Some sessions were longer than others, so I'd bring some humorous videos or CDs to listen to with her. At times we were quiet, yet there was no discomfort or awkwardness about the silence. It was a healing time, a praying time, a gift that the two of us shared.

I remember people asking me, "what do you do all of that time in the infusion center? Do you run out of things to talk about?" My answer was simple, "We do whatever feels right at the time. We do not have a planned agenda. We just remain present to one another."

Today was an important day—it was Nan's final chemotherapy. I was uptight because I had to attend a meeting outside of the hospital, and I did not want to be late for her last session. As luck would have it, it was a dreary, rainy day. I wanted to do something special to celebrate her accomplishment. On my way back to the hospital I pulled into a strip mall where I saw a florist's sign and bought her a colorful bouquet of flowers and congratulation balloons.

Since this was to be her last chemo, I expected her to be happy and somewhat relaxed. She definitely was not. I could see the stress on her face, which was also reflected in her eyes. She thanked me for the flowers, and a nurse arrived to set up her chemo. I walked out of the room, as I always did, so that she could have her privacy. As I strolled the halls, I wondered what was going on. I prayed for guidance when I returned to the room.

Nan appeared a little more settled, as I began our usual routine. I turned on the soft music, reclined her chair back and elevated her feet on the bolster. I began with a breathing meditation and then slipped into the reflexology session with the guided imagery and energy healing. At completion, I also balanced her Chakras. Now Nan appeared very relaxed.

We sat in silence for a long time. The peace and positive energy were delightful. Slowly, Nan began to share her thoughts with me. That's when I realized that although this was a day for celebrating, it was also a very scary time. Without the chemo to fight the disease, would the cancer return? Every time she felt an ache or pain, would she attribute it to the cancer? How do you pick up the pieces and continue the journey? Only time will tell!

THE CROWN CHAKRA

"What lies behind us and what lies before us are tiny
matters compared to what lies within us."
~ Ralph Waldo Emerson

The seventh chakra is our spiritual connector. It allows our spirituality to become an integral part of our physical lives and guide us. Our life energy radiates the light of being, and being is the field of all possibilities. This chakra is located at the crown of the head, and the color is a shimmering violet.

While our energy system as a whole is animated by our spirit, the crown chakra is directly aligned to seek an intimate relationship with the Divine. We learn that enlightenment is not out of reach. We need to experience self-awareness and presence to be fully alive in the moment. Radical change is not necessary for this to happen. These moments are present to us daily, if we go within and seek. All of the answers are anxiously waiting in each of us as we watch the sun rise in the quiet of morning or view the stars dancing in the sky at the end of day. The invitation is…Be still and know that I am here.

I Believe in Angels...
Nancy Holecek

"Coincidences can be small miracles."

I was not prepared for my cancer diagnosis and, like most, it hit me like a ton of bricks. *How could this be happening to me*???? I was 40 years old, the working mother of two toddlers, and way too busy and young to be dealing with this. Having just lost both parents to cancer, this seemed like a cruel joke.

As a nurse, I was used to being the doer, the caregiver, the healer. I was *not* used to being taken care of, nor was that easy for me to accept. I was the strong one.

Until now...

And that was how my journey began—my journey of surgery, chemotherapy, reconstruction, endless radiation treatments, more surgery, and the introduction to a new body image. And finally, my healing came and I was starting from a brand new reference point.

So that was the tough part of my journey. But there were blessed parts too.

How was I to know, when I was walking out of the doctor's office on the day of diagnosis, that I would run in to an old friend and co-worker who would turn out to be my angel and my miracle?

Lynn Ferrer is my angel here on earth. And she's not just *my* angel; she's one to so many of us whose lives she has touched. She is a humble, selfless, caring healer. She is empowered by her faith and by the love and compassion in her heart. She was and is my mother, my friend, my rock. She taught me to be open, to receive, and to have faith.

She began her ministry with AIDS patients—mostly homosexuals or drug users—at a time when little was known about the disease and the sick were regarded as outcasts. Her compassion and concern for their plight motivated her to start a support group which grew to weekend retreats and in turn led Lynn to venture further down her path—*her* journey to become a healer. Already a nurse, she studied holistic and integrative care, became a Reiki Master, and began working in the cancer center, her own office, her home, and in her patients' homes as necessary.

Lynn is gentle. Her hugs are full of love, her voice is soothing, her meditations transport, and her hands are warm and radiate energy.

I have felt the presence of God in *her* presence. I have felt her healing touch and have received her blessings.

She taught me it is OK to receive and to let others care for me. She said that allowing someone to care for another is a gift for both the recipient *and* the giver.

I cannot begin to imagine the number of lives she has touched, but I know there are many. I am so grateful that one of them was mine. She is beloved. I have been truly blessed beyond measure to know her. She is my miracle...my angel. This is my tribute to Lynn and my thank-you to her.

Standing Strong
Diane Braschi

*"We are each of us angels with one wing, and we can
only fly by embracing each other."*
~ Luciano de Crescenzo

Death and loss have been a huge part of my being.
Since I was a young girl, I have tragically lost too many
close friends and relatives—cousins dying from accidents
and disease, losing friends to drugs and cancer, losing my
only sibling to a gunshot, and losing my father-in-law and
husband to untimely, senseless tragedies. All too young
and all too full of life.

On a bright, sunny Sunday morning in May I said
goodbye to my husband, not knowing that it would be the
last time I would ever see him alive. That morning he
suffered a fatal fall, leaving me a widow at the age of 44
and our three children fatherless at ages nine, thirteen, and
fifteen. My children were my salvation through the
mourning and grief. They were my strength, and I knew I
had to be strong for them. I thought if they saw that I was
OK, they would be OK. I used to say I would "fake it
until I made it." It was my mission to let them know we
could still have happy lives. I wanted them to grow up
hopeful, not bitter, fearful, and sad. Our lives were
forever changed, but I knew we had the strength within us
to rise above our fear and sadness.

I tried not to miss a beat and did everything I could to
keep our lives "normal", the way it used to be. I stayed
involved in the schools, worked, volunteered, took them

on trips, celebrated their many achievements, and just kept moving forward, never missing a beat. Relationships changed; some family and friends disappeared while new, strong bonds formed. My children grew and flourished into wonderful young adults.

In 2009, just four years after my husband died, I was faced with a diagnosis of rectal cancer. I was overcome with fear and felt so alone. How was I going to explain this to my children? I could not even focus on the cancer because I was too distraught thinking about how my children would react. I kept my diagnosis a secret from everyone except a few close friends who accompanied me through the exhaustive tests. Fearing the reaction of my children, I rehearsed what I would say, knowing I needed to put a positive spin on this to ease their worry and pain. It was the hardest thing I ever had to do aside from telling them that their father had died.

After my first surgery, I was told that there were lymph nodes involved and that I would be having both chemotherapy and radiation. I was so frightened and could not share my feelings with my children, parents, or even friends. The fear of dying and leaving my children without parents was too much to bear. They had been through too much already and I felt so guilty burdening them with more. For the first time in my life, I felt crippled with fear and hopelessness.

It was at this time, when all my thoughts were about dying, that I met Brother Paul, a servant of God. It was at that meeting that I knew I was not alone. Brother Paul prayed for me and blessed me. I sobbed like never before, finally letting go of all my fears. At that moment I felt the grace of God and the power of prayer. I turned to God and gave Him all my fears and worries. Since then, I have felt a warm inner peace. This sounds crazy, even to me!

Even though I was raised as a Catholic and am a

product of twelve years of Catholic education, I never felt really connected to God. It was hard for me to believe in God when my own life and the lives of so many people I loved were devastated by tragedy. Through Brother Paul I met so many inspiring, spiritual people with unwavering faith. They have comforted me and shown me how a life with God in it is the only way to live. I am eternally grateful for their friendship and encouragement.

And then I met Lynn, a holistic nurse who is the most spiritual, faith-filled, beautiful, and loving person. Lynn possesses an easy, nurturing, positive quality which makes me believe that I can and will get through anything and come out whole on the other side. She has helped me see the power of faith and spirituality and how I can use the gifts I possess to help others.

I was hesitant when Lynn first asked me to be part of a cancer support group for women; what qualified me to help others? I have walked in their shoes. I know the fear and isolation that a cancer diagnosis brings. I wanted to share my story and let others know that they too can survive this with grace and hope. We each walk our own path, but in the end it is a blessing to share it with such courageous, amazing women.

I do believe things happen for a reason and that I probably will never know the reason for my cancer. My life has affected so many people, and so many lives have had a profound effect on me. It is mind-boggling to discover that the very people I am most inspired by are inspired by me! Imagine that! I am so fortunate to be surrounded by positive, loving friends. I am continually inspired by the courage of the women I meet through WINGS. I do not want to be defined by my cancer, but it has changed me in more ways than just physically. I have chosen Faith over Fear and Hope over Hopelessness.

THE BROW/THIRD EYE CHAKRA

"Intuition is a sense of knowing how to act spontaneously without needing to know why." ~ *Sylvia Clare*

We each have an inner voice to navigate our life's path. Visualize this energy as a beautiful gift and align yourself with your sixth chakra. The color is an indigo blue, and it is located between your eyebrows in the center of your forehead.

This chakra is not a magical or healing gift for only certain individuals. The truth is that it is part of our real self. Intuition comes alive when we listen deeply and awakens and invites a powerful shift in our lives. Intuition that speaks to us is the ultimate wisdom of the Universe.

When you ignore your intuition and make a fast decision without allowing the time and space to move inside and listen to your inner voice, you'll always end up in trouble. Going within to that peaceful place is the answer. There, we can gently and lovingly move in the direction that is best for us. By opening the flow of receptivity and our innate guiding power, we access a calm, mindful presence that gives us a clear sense of what is in our highest and best good.

Stage 5, Anyone?
Rena Cooper

I'll start by confessing that I know there is no stage 5 in cancer speak. My journey began at stage 4. Stages 1, 2, and 3 had slipped by undetected by my doctors and me.

Part I

Unless you've been there, it's hard to grasp what it feels like to get a cancer diagnosis, let alone stage 4. It was a combination of shock, terror, anger, and disbelief. I had been cheated!! Where was MY stage 1? *You know, that's the one with all the hope surrounding it.* The one that when you finish chemo, you can't wait to tell everyone, "I'm cancer free!"

What had I been doing with my life while stages 1, 2, and 3 were partying inside me? Thinking back, I had just retired from teaching and was anxiously trying to plan what my new life would be. The possibilities seemed endless! Then I hit a bump in the road. It actually tuned out to be a major pothole. Why was I spotting at age 62? Two doctors, one of whom was a gynecologist specializing in cancer, two D&Cs, and several ultrasounds later, I was relieved to be diagnosed with a hormonal imbalance. *Bye-bye stages 1, 2, AND 3.*

Six months later, in December 2008, I was STILL spotting. Some survival instinct FINALLY kicked in. I took my medical records and went to see a third specialist. He looked at my records and said, "This has nothing to do with your hormones." Later that same day, I had the first of what would become many CAT scans. It confirmed a uterine tumor. My surgeon was optimistic, and so was I. *A residue of stage 1 left behind?* The tumor would be completely removed, and that would be the end of it. I would continue on with my life as before. *Remember, "I'm cancer free!"?*

Unfortunately, my surgeon appeared in the recovery room, looking like the grim reaper minus the sickle. He told me that my cancer had metastasized, and that I would need to start chemotherapy immediately. He couldn't look me in the eyes. I had gone from zero to sixty on the Cancer Speedway in the time it took to remove all parts feminine.

What, if anything, should I do now? And so began my cancer journey. First stop, Sloan Kettering. *Harps playing, heavens parting.* Surely they could help me.

Part II

It was a cold rainy night in January of 2009 when Gary and I headed to the Mecca of the cancer world. As instructed, I carried along my medical records and pathology slides. The young oncologist I was assigned to entered the exam room after going over my records. He sat across from us, and in full "boo-boo" face with lower lip protruding, delivered the bad news. "You have a stage 4 cancer that is incurable." That was his opening line. He went on to say something about some women doing chemotherapy, and the "lucky" ones getting some remission time. I heard very little of anything else he said. *Something to do with flu like side effects.* My brain had left the building. I just couldn't get past the doctor's face and hearing the words, "stage 4 cancer".

My story might have ended there if it hadn't been for the persistence of my surgeon. *Remember the guy minus the sickle?* He insisted on my getting a second opinion. So, with the help of my husband, I staggered into the cancer center at St. Barnabas, white-faced and weepy. This time I met with a female oncologist who took a totally different approach. She convinced me that many women live a long time with uterine cancer—six years and counting! Hanging on to her confident lab coat tails, I agreed to do treatment. I had gone in with no hope and left two hours later hanging on to a glimmer.

Of course, talking about doing treatment and actually doing it are two different things. Somehow, with my husband Gary's support, I made it to the cancer center that first day. My terror was visible...but guess what? I did it!

Two angels, both named Lynn, came to my rescue that day. One Lynn was my oncology nurse. She sat with me and helped me to feel safe. The second Lynn was the holistic nurse at the cancer center. You can imagine my surprise when she cleared my little room—my bug–eyed, protective Gary included—dimmed the lights, put on beautiful music, took out beautiful smelling oils and gave me the best foot massage of my life! *Will I have to pay for this?* She did all the reflexology points on my feet while I dozed on and off in my recliner. When I got home that day, I couldn't wait to call friends and family and tell them what a wonderful experience chemo had been. "Foot massage! Did you have to pay for it?" Maybe this wasn't going to be as bad as I thought.

Two days later, I could barely get out of bed.

My treatment went on for more than 6 months. My husband drove me to St. Barnabas every three weeks and stayed with me the entire time. He also took off from his painting business rather than leave me alone in the house. We bonded in a way that made me love him even more. *Impossible!*

Things were going along relatively well—*relative to what, the plague?*—until I completed three of the six treatments. One morning, after brushing my teeth, I went to spit out the water, and it dribbled down my chest! It was just like when you have Novocain at the dentist, and he tells you to rinse. Not pretty! After doing a quick inventory of my head for leaks, I realized my head was intact, but my neck had me in a half-Nelson. I couldn't bend it downward or upward. My oncologist concluded that there was a tiny metastatic spot on my cervical spine. So chemo stopped while I did ten radiation treatments. It was successful, and I no longer need a bib to brush my teeth.

Unfortunately, I had to do an extra chemo treatment to make up for the month I had to take off for the radiation. Gradually, I recovered my strength and blessedly, drifted into remission. I was one of the "lucky" ones. *Remember the doc at MSK?*

At this point, most survivors would never want to step foot into a cancer center again, other than for checkups. However, Lynn, the holistic nurse, had other plans. She invited a group of women cancer patients to attend an all-day Reiki workshop at the hospital corporate center. I was delighted to be invited. Lynn had been doing Reiki on me along with the foot reflexology. This was an opportunity to learn how to do it on myself and others. Although I had just finished my last treatment that week and wasn't feeling so hot, I was determined to be part of it.

What a feeling I got when I walked into the room! Every woman attending, me included, was wearing a wig, a bandana, or a scarf on their head! I wasn't alone! *I had peeps!* Lynn had arranged the program to give us ample time to sit, chat, and bond in between the instruction. By the end of the day, not only could we do Reiki, we had made new friends. Friends that felt like sisters after one day! Phone numbers and e-mails were exchanged with promises of lunch dates.

Part III

Over time, with Lynn's encouragement, a group of us came together that shared her vision. Women touched by cancer need a place to interact with other women going through the same experience. Our mission became to give emotional support and information that would help all of us live better lives. *Remember the impact that Reiki class had?* Over a year of breakfasts, brunches, and lunches, we began to believe that we had the power to bring it to life. Welcome to the world, WINGS!...Women Inspiring, Nurturing, and Giving Strength and Support.

Five years later, I feel so proud and blessed by what WINGS has accomplished. Our monthly programs have been a great success. We've learned Reiki, QiGong, TaiChi, healing movement, drumming, healthy cooking, meditation, writing for healing, and so much more. Each meeting is followed by a sharing circle where members can share or just listen. Sometimes there are tears, but more often than not there is laughter. Everyone leaves with a smile on their face. Just being with women you know understand and respect your feelings does so much to lift our spirits.

Now I know you must be asking, how did all this lead me to stage 5? After all of the knowledge and healthy practices I had followed, along with an amazing support system, *love my peeps*, my cancer came out of a 5 ½ year remission. It was almost 6 years since my last treatment, and now I was starting over again. With the support of my family, friends, and WINGS sisters, I made it through eighteen weekly treatments. The foot massages were a huge help! *I love you, Lynn.*

Now I am determined to get at least another 6 years. I have the confidence that comes from being part of something bigger than me. I'm needed to help carry on our WINGS mission! With that in mind, I know I have possibly a few more "stages" left in me. Call them "lives" if you want—it works for my cats, why not me?

The Flapping of My Little Wings
Joni Jasterzbski

In recent years, I learned about the Butterfly Effect and its application to all living things. In 1963, a scientist named Edward Lorenz hypothesized that a butterfly's wings could set molecules in motion, pushing other molecules that eventually would snowball into a blizzard or hurricane on the other side of the planet. This law of physics applies to all matter, including people. I am only one person, but the constant flapping of my little wings has made a positive difference in the lives of many.

I have always had a strong sixth sense and I trust my instincts. On September 11, 2001, I awoke around five a.m. from a nightmare that a massive airplane had crashed into the Twin Towers. In the dream, the towers exploded and crumbled down into ashes. Little did I know that only a few hours later this nightmare would become a reality. I was horrified and found out that I knew children who had lost their fathers in the tragedy. I felt the need to do something…anything.

I am an artist, so I designed patriotic pins in 77 styles, mass-produced them, and sold them for six dollars each. There was no advertising for this project except word of mouth, hardworking hands, and generous hearts. We raised $25,000 in eighteen months by selling 4,016 pins throughout the U.S. and Europe. My original goal was $500. This act of kindness grew much bigger than my original intention and was a testament to the inherent goodness of people. God gave me the talent to make a difference and blessed me with the tenacity to carry it out.

Not long after the tragedy, a firefighter found out about the pins and asked me to paint a massive banner to honor the 343 firemen who lost their lives. This banner was hung at memorial services and was later carried up Mount Washington for a fundraiser by the firefighters. These men and women raised $10,000 in two days for children of the lost firemen. I believe that God showed me the avenue to be able to do the most good.

In 2008, I was diagnosed with stage 3 breast cancer. I was shocked and very saddened that the cancer treatments would force me to take a leave of absence from the job I loved so much. I have been an elementary school art teacher for 30 years in Verona Public Schools. Throughout the chemo, mastectomy, reconstruction, and radiation, my most pervasive thought was surviving and being healthy for my family. My strong motivation to return back to work helped in my survival like dominos falling into place.

After eight arduous months of infusion treatments, surgery, rehab, and radiation, I received a beautifully painted ceramic heart of hope with a sweet get-well message from a third-grade student. There was a pretty little flower on it and wishes for a quick recovery. I was blown away with this little creation and immediately realized that I wanted to get involved in the organization that had sent it.

I contacted Hearts of Hope when I got home and was rolling, cutting, stamping, and painting hearts three days later. I proposed this community service project to my schools and we have been painting and handing the hearts out to a local hospital ever since. To date, I have painted and overseen the creation of more than 5,000 hearts of hope. I was their volunteer of the year in 2010, and in 2014 I was selected to be one of six people in the U.S. to be awarded the Ambassador of Hope Award. My older students have brought the program to Verona High School, where they create 500 hearts each year. My former students who are now teachers themselves brought the program to their schools and have created hundreds more.

Hearts of Hope were even sent down to Newtown, Connecticut, after the school shooting. Afterwards, Newtown sent them to the people in Boston after the marathon bombing. Following this, Boston created a chapter and sent the hearts to Prescott, Arizona, in honor of the lost firefighters; they then made them for the tornado victims in Moore, Oklahoma, and now all of these cities are making them for the Wounded Warrior Project. There are also Hearts for Heroes that I have made and sent for troops in Iraq and Afghanistan as well as veterans throughout the U.S.

One idea and the need to make a difference can create a wave of goodness. I truly believe that kindness is contagious. One good intention can evolve into a mass pay-it-forward. Mahatma Ghandi said, "Be the change you wish to see in the world." I am doing this through teaching, community service, by being a part of the Hearts of Hope organization, and by my involvement in a non-profit women's cancer support group called WINGS.

The catalyst for WINGS was an amazing holistic nurse, Lynn Ferrer from St. Barnabas Hospital, who urged a group of former patients to create a support group for women with cancer. There were nine of us and we formed WINGS – Women Inspiring Nurturing and Giving Strength and Support. Our mission is to help alleviate stress through the healing arts. Our group has been reaching out to women for five years, and we are making a real difference.

We all have the power to make a change. By your

hand, lives can be altered and caught up in a chain of much larger events. The very beating of your heart has meaning and purpose. Your life and what you choose to do with it matters and will affect the future. I have been blessed with so many incredible people and artistic talents, and I will continue to pay it forward.

There is no doubt in my mind that performing these various acts of kindness and flapping my little wings helped to pull me through this life-changing ordeal called cancer. The warmth of people fed my soul, spirit, and mind, and carried me through a very difficult experience. Creativity, love, and kindness define me, not cancer. I have new eyes to see, a new lease on living, and I have never felt so alive.

THE THROAT CHAKRA

*"Nobody cares if you can't dance well,
just get up and dance."* ~ *Martha Graham*

How we express ourselves is an integral part of spiritual growth. It is an extension of the way we approach life and speak our truth. When we hold back our truth, we limit our joy. What we put out into the Universe is what we receive back. This is the story of the fifth chakra. The color is a light blue, and it is located in the center of the throat.

When we begin to give voice to our dreams, we are a step closer to actualizing them. Through our words and actions, we become what we feel, what we say, and how we express ourselves. Each expression is unique and powerful—this is our reality. In activating the throat chakra, we allow the flow of freedom, inspiration, and boldness, which gives voice to our dreams. Who we are and how we express ourselves adds to the creative flow of the Universe.

What I Carry
Rena Cooper

I carry my healing
in my cloth shopping bags.
Home from the food store
with my soon to be
elixir of nutrients.

Bring on the kale, the carrots,
the beets and asparagus!
Toss in some cucumber and celery.
Cut off a tiny piece of ginger…for kicks.

I gently drop my precious organic cargo
into the chute of my beloved juicer.
Grind away, sweet chariot!
Change nature's garden into my healing,
and carry ME back to health.

Overwhelmed
Holly Whitmore Denton

Overwhelmed.

Waiting. Waiting. Waiting.

Fear.

Diagnosis.

FEAR.

DARKNESS.

Vocabulary. Doctors.

Surgery.

LOSS.

Chemotherapy.

LOSS.

Hair. Sexuality. Self Esteem.

Medications.

Tears.

Side Effects.

Tears.

Family.

LOVE.

Friends. Support. Love.

Strangers. Love.

Prayers. Love.

Food. Food. Food.

GIFTS.

Prayer.

GOD.

Communion.

Blessings.

GRACE.

LOVE.

GRACE. LIGHT.

LOVE. LOVE. LOVE.

OVERWHELMED!

Me
Randi E. Jeddis

I used to be small, but now I'm not

I used to have a weak voice, but now I don't

I used to have myopic vision, but now I don't

I used to be the underdog, but now I'm not

I used to be afraid, but now I'm not

I was never supposed to be anything, but now I am

I have found peace and strength in beating the odds

and fooling them all

Sisters
Randi E. Jeddis

Just because we have the same mother
does not mean we are sisters

Just because my father became your father
does not mean we are sisters

Just because half of our DNA is the same
does not mean we are sisters

Just because your children are my niece and nephews
does not mean we are

Sisters.

What meant we were sisters
was the laughter and the tears

What meant we were sisters
was taking the good with the bad

What meant we were sisters
was the ability to honor, understand, protect and
lean on each other.

We are no longer sisters…

You tell me why.

THE HEART CHAKRA

*"Your task is not to seek for love, but merely to seek
and find all the barriers within yourself
that you have built against it."* ~ Ruminate

The fourth chakra is the central powerhouse of the human energy system. It is located in the center of the chest, and the color is an emerald green. It mediates between the body and spirit and determines their health and strength. Loving oneself as a fourth chakra challenge means having the courage to listen to the heart's emotional messages and spiritual directions. We continue the journey by activating that part of our life energy that is precious, potent, and could be the nectar of our human experience.

Love is compassionate and forgiving, and it unites even as it celebrates differences.

When we open the heart chakra to compassion and love, we feel connected and whole. What happens in our lives is that the more we give, the more we receive. Our lives get better and better. Gratitude activates the energy of love. The heart chakra embodies the spiritual lesson that teaches us how to act out of love and compassion. The most powerful energy we have is love.

Beatrice
Randi E. Jeddis

I watched a butterfly die today.

My sorrow shifted to amazement as I watched her flutter her last flutters, as opposed to her first flight.

I was awed by her beauty, dignity, grace and strength.

I prayed with her and I prayed for her.

Did she feel my love? I gave her as much of the day's last sun before night came and robbed the warmth and turned it cold. The temperature dipped, the sun set, and she fluttered softer and softer. Her wings came together like two hands applauding for a job well done and a life well lived. Her wing's closed one final time. Her work on earth was done.

Stillness and peace took her place.

Go in peace my sentient being and continue your work wherever it takes you. May you take flight in another life, a flight you could not take in this life. Despite your challenges and deformities the majesty of your deep penetrating colors lit up the room.

Even in death as you struggled, your radiance was still present.

We are taught to think that eleven days of life in this world is not enough time. Perhaps the teaching is that sometimes and in some cases it may be just right. The lesson is less about time, but rather who and what we touch and who and what we let touch us, especially when our wings are damaged.

Go in peace dear Beatrice, suffer no more.

I watched a butterfly die today.

Beyond My Wildest Expectations
Holly Whitmore Denton

I was diagnosed with breast cancer in October 2008. October. Really? Breast Cancer Awareness month? OK. I get it. I really get it. I have it. I had it. I am fully aware.

But I must say that after the scary and hard day of diagnosis something incredible happened almost every day from then on.

Of course there were lots of hard days, scary days, painful days, sleepless days, anxiety-filled and nauseous days too. But just about every day there was something— a card, a call, an email, a gesture—that lifted me and carried me through. Sometimes they were grand and magnificent, but many times it was the (seemingly) smallest kindness that had my eyes filled with tears of amazement, joy, and gratitude.

Cancer made me face my mortality. I couldn't look at my children at the beginning without crying and feeling ill. It was the unknown. My mind did not comprehend much of anything but fear.

Of course we all will die someday—I knew this. But I thought I was still young and my children were young and my beloved husband . . .

I didn't know if I was going to die from this disease or not, but I was in a very dark place. I had never felt truly depressed before, but that is what it felt like. Dark, depressed and very scared. At times I could hardly speak.

Hearing the word cancer next to your name is a gut

punch like no other.

But people surrounded me with all kinds of love. And I let them. Perhaps it sounds cliché or "Hallmark-like"...no matter. It was this way for me. It was hard to let go and allow people to help me, and I had to force myself to do that sometimes. I felt like I was losing control of my life in many ways—losing so many things, but people swarmed in and swaddled me with love.

And I thought I understood love at least a little, but this daily (sometimes hourly) onslaught of caring, loving, selfless gestures and kindnesses were beyond comprehension.

My mother-in-law arrived and stayed to help for two weeks after my surgery. It was two weeks before Christmas. She has 11 children and 25 grandchildren, so she had just a bit of holiday shopping, organizing, and cooking to do, but where was she? At our house with a huge smile on her face at all times.

My friends organized meals for us for months, they walked our dog, shuttled my children, showered me with gifts, sang songs, drove me to appointments, washed my hair, offered to do our laundry(!), and countless other things.

Homemade soup arrived every other day for my lunches, and another delivery of soup came on Sundays for whenever we needed it. Spectacular meals arrived daily for our dinner. The food never stopped!

One day, a meal arrived from someone we were not expecting. I was resting and my mother-in–law answered the door. The note said it was from my oldest son's chemistry teacher, who I had seen exactly once (but never really met) at back-to-school night. She had never met me. She listed all the ingredients of her lovely homemade meal, "in case anyone might be allergic." She then went on to say, "I imagine it is hard when the mom is down for a while. I hope this helps a little." There was a PS on the bottom that told me not to worry about Jack (my son) because she was keeping a special eye on him for me.

We all couldn't get over that. What a beautiful person—how unbelievably kind. I didn't even know her.

The nurses and staff at the Cancer center were truly angelic—and still are. They treated me so tenderly, with such loving gentleness. They were another amazing and caring force that carried me through the tougher days.

I called a woman whose name had been given to me by my surgeon's office staff. She was going to talk to me and share about her surgery experience, etc. She was incredibly helpful and so nice. She went through and explained exactly what was going to happen to me. It was a particularly hard day when I called her, and she literally lifted me from the lowest dark place to a calmer and less fearful state of mind. She asked me for the date of my surgery at the end of our conversation, and after I told her the date she said, "I wanted it to put on my calendar so I can pray for you that day." Incredible. A stranger will pray for me.

These were the kinds of things that occurred throughout my journey and they made me feel cradled, held, and loved each step of the way.

My children and my husband were amazing—my husband especially. But they were also scared. And all of these things helped them too. What a life lesson for my kids to see how to help people when they are going through hard times.

Another acquaintance of mine offered to bring me to be blessed by a "very holy man" before my surgery. I just happen to mention this offer to my doctor. She knew this "holy man." I was planning to go and receive this blessing, (why wouldn't I?) but after hearing my scientist surgeon endorse it and tell me to go, there was no way I would have not gone.

I was profoundly moved by that blessing experience. It literally changed my life.

So would I ever wish cancer on anyone?

Absolutely never.

But what has happened in my life since my cancer is beyond my wildest expectations. It has been an incredible acknowledgement and re-affirmation of human kindness and God's love.

At the End of the World...
Rena Cooper

Call me to a quiet place.

Surround me with the things

and people I love.

Let me gather them in my arms.

Lots of kisses, licks, and purrs.

And let me close my eyes

and pass quietly away

to that place where all is good...

No fears, no pain,

and no regret.

THE SOLAR PLEXUS CHAKRA

"All the powers of the universe are already ours."
~ Swami Vivekananda

The third chakra is our personal power center, the magnetic core of the personality and ego. This is the center of personal power in relation to the external world. The color is a brilliant shade of gold, like the sun. It assists us further in the process of individuation, of forming a "self" ego and personality separate from our inherited families. It is our channel of self-esteem. Power can be misunderstood, since it is often used to hurt people. Energy from this chakra balances power within us, which allows the flow of energy to connect to what we want and provides the power to attain it.

You have the power to achieve the things that matter most to you. Divine power, true power, comes from compassion and love, which are gifts from within. That is why it is so important to stay in touch with your inner being.

My Deal
Terry Meier

One day, I made a deal with God,
right there outside the hospital entrance door…
This day wasn't an ordinary day.
I had a doctor's appointment and a test; a 'lump' test.

I woke up that morning
and had my favorite, soothing cup of tea.
I got dressed –
even took time for make-up and my hair and off I went.
I didn't need anyone with me;
I could handle this appointment alone.
I drove east on Route 78 to a 'wannabe' thriving city.
But this city and its' people seem unable to move forward
from their individual differences and financial hardships.

I parked my Volvo in a parking lot monitored by hospital
security and walked toward the hospital entrance door.
Once passing through this door, meeting the doctor, and
completing my 'lump' test…

I knew two things:
The test result could drastically change my life
or
I could continue along my path in my little world.

Before I opened the hospital door, a woman approached
me.

She was shabbily dressed with a big, old black coat
and well worn shoes...
clothes not enough to keep her warm.
She explained she'd been sick
and hadn't eaten in a few days.

Then the question...
I knew the question before she spoke it.
"Could you spare money for a chicken dinner
at that store on the corner?
It doesn't cost much."

There was the moment -
staring right at me -
my opportunity to make a deal -
to make a deal with God.

A screaming started in my head.
Everything I knew and learned throughout my life
from my mom and dad, family, friends, teachers
and even acquaintances said
"Nooooo! God doesn't make deals."

So I asked, "God,
if I give this hungry, desperate woman money to eat,
would you allow my 'lump' test to be negative?"

I did it.
I gave her money and walked through the hospital door.

Was God in the deal making business?

I had to give it a shot!

Didn't I?

Invisible
Holly Whitmore Denton

Three weeks after my surgery, it was my youngest son's tenth birthday. He and I had decided that his friends would come over for cake and then my husband would take them to a movie. That was all I could manage. I was just happy I was dressed and out of bed.

I was holding the door open as the boys streamed in for the party. One father was making his way down our walkway. I said hello to him.

He looked past me to my husband who was about twelve feet behind me in the kitchen doorway and said hello to him. I thought, hmmm…that was kind of odd.

I tried again. "Hi, Mike."

Once again he avoided looking at me and asked my husband by name how he was. He then walked past me into my house, never making eye contact or responding to me.

I was in shock. I had never been invisible before, but in that moment that is exactly how I felt.

Invisible.

Holy crow. Is this how it was going to be now? Is this because I had my breasts removed? Is this because the word "BREAST" is in the phrase "Breast Cancer???"

I was literally standing there trying to figure out what had just happened.

He was embarrassed to look at me. Why…because he didn't know where to look? Because he was afraid to ask how I was?

At that time, it was a very dramatic encounter for me.

Going forward this would happen here and there but not in such an obvious or in "in my face" way. Most of the time it happened with men, and they would just avoid eye contact. And like most things it became less and less frequent over time.

It happened with women too, but for different reasons. Some people just don't know what to say, or they feel uncomfortable with your disease or surgery or whatever hard thing you are coping with, so they avoid you. That would upset me now and then, but truth be told, sometimes it was a relief.

Everyone was expecting me to "move on" now, and so many things had dramatically changed—both physically and in so many other ways.

I was starting to understand that this was actually just the beginning of a totally new phase of my journey.

THE SACRAL CHAKRA

"Happiness is what you think, what you say, and what you do are in harmony." ~ Mahatma Gandhi

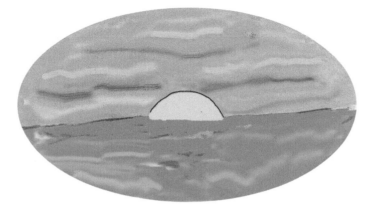

The activation of the second chakra brings the free-flowing energy of happiness and joy. This chakra is located 2 inches below the navel, and the color is a glorious shade of orange. The sacral chakra deals with our one-on-one relationships, the comfort of our sexuality, our control issues, and our financial security. When open, this energy center allows us to recognize that our true desires are cues that lead us to happiness, creativity, a sense of delight, and bliss.

When we focus on our dreams and desires, we will be guided to a state of pleasure and serenity. Desire is a divine gift. It motivates us to get up each morning and live each day to the fullest. Without the spirit of desire, life would be flat and colorless.

Hair I Am
Rena Cooper

I cannot recall when I first became aware of having hair on my head. My baby pictures show me as an almost bald infant, followed quickly by a skinny little girl with chin-length, semi-curly brown hair. I gave no thought to my hair, and my hair and I lived in harmony. That lasted through most of elementary school. And then it began. I suddenly found myself immersed in a tug of war with my tresses that would last for almost sixty years.

Lest I mislead my reader, I must confess that I never really had "tresses". That was the hair of fairy tale girls. I longed for long, shiny tresses, but DNA and MOM would have none of it. My hair had to be kept short and manageable. It was easier for a busy mother with limited hair skills to maintain. My princess hair would have to remain *in* my head, not *on* it. However, no one could have predicted the twists and turns that were about to become part of my hair history.

My life seemed to be going along smoothly when I suddenly developed the nervous habit of hair twirling. That's when you take one finger of your personal choice and twirl several strands of hair around said finger until it becomes knotted to the scalp. This process could usually be reversed with time and patience, but not always. Sometimes the knot didn't want to let go. That's when the comb became a medieval torture device in my mother's hands. If my hair didn't want to let go, the scissors were employed. Favorite times for twirling were when watching TV, reading, or riding in a car. In today's psychology terms, this would fall under the heading of "self-soothing". It's right up there with thumb-sucking, but much less visible.

Over time, the desire to grow longer hair curtailed my twirling habits. My mother now took to braiding my hair. These were my "Heidi" days. I had a braid on each side of my head that formed a loop in front of each ear. Thank heaven I was a huge Heidi fan and happy to look like her. She might not have been a princess, but my hair could do Heidi. It was never going to do Rapunzel. Mom was just happy I had stopped twirling. However, since I didn't look like any of the other girls in my grade level, the braids would have to go. I was finally ready to take charge of my own hair life.

Hair We Go

I headed into my teen years like most females in the '60s. The boys called it "helmet head". My friends and I all sported oversized heads of hair. The bigger the do, the better. This was achieved by "teasing" the hair with a fine comb. It left us all looking like we had been electrocuted. It was actually very similar to my twirling. It was the next step that created the magic. With practice, the top layer could be made smooth. The final step was to blast the whole thing with industrial strength hair spray—twice. Our hairdos lasted for days. Sleeping was a bit challenging, and caution needed to be taken before embracing an elderly person or small child. It was not unheard of to cause bodily harm by accidently colliding with a helmet head. There was more than one documented case of a boyfriend chipping a tooth when going in for a sneak kiss.

A great way to add even more body to the hair before

teasing was to set the hair on large rollers. Empty soup cans would do in a pinch. Since we did not yet have the luxury of Velcro back then, bobby pins would hold them in place. You could go to bed and let time dry it. Or you could sit under your portable hooded dryer for an hour. The former made it almost impossible to get any sleep, and the latter left your scalp branded like a steer with little bobby pin burn marks. Are we having fun yet?

Mercifully, things began to ease up over the next several years. I still fought the good fight, trying to look more like Marlo Thomas than Richard Simmons. Some days I was more successful than others. A lot depended on the humidity. My salvation came in the form of a hand-held hair blower and those fabulous Velcro rollers. I could now get passable results and felt more confident in how I looked. Other popular inventions came along like the curling iron. I could never use it without burning my scalp. Each time I would throw the bleeping thing out. They were cheap, and it was a release for some of my frustration. I have purchased at least five curling irons in my life. No mas.

The unanswered question you should be asking me right now is, "Did you ever make peace with your hair?" The answer would be, "Yes!" but not in a way that I could have ever predicted. After sporting the same style and color for more than 20 years, I was in for the most dramatic hair change of my life. Having been diagnosed with cancer in 2008, I now had to brace myself for losing my nemesis to chemotherapy drugs. After my initial shock and hysteria, I accepted the new me and bought a wig. That's when I learned my first big hair lesson. It's easier to live without hair than with it. Those wig months were bliss. Both my confidence and self-image soared. I held out hope that when it grew back in, I'd be one of those people who wind up with totally different hair.

Didn't happen. Every wave, curl, and cowlick was back!

Hair Not Required

In 2014, after having a second recurrence of my cancer, I was required to undergo radiation to my head. This time, when my hair grew back in, everything about it was different. Not better, just different. It is now the color of Brillo, and the texture of fried wool. I have classic male-pattern baldness, thin on top and cradle cap in the back. It's a look sported by many of the men we love but not accepted in women. So it's back to the wig, this time for good. I think I'll get a new one. I've earned a new perfect hairstyle. Perhaps it's time for a long, straight Suzanne Somers look. Is it too late for Rapunzel?

I'll end my hair odyssey with a question for my reader. "Where's the money?!" I keep rooting through my pocketbook searching for a loose $20 bill. The money I'm not spending on my hair has to be somewhere! I was spending $70 a month for color, $60 every eight weeks for a cut, and at least $30 a month for hair products. Add to that another $20 a year on those "bleeping" curling irons. I repeat, "Where's the money?"

Eventually, I will find a pile of money in a pocketbook that I haven't used in a while. Until then, life is good. We just need to show up and look interested. Hair not required. It's about being able to look inside ourselves and see the perfect person that we are.

It's not about the hair. It never was.

Catch a Ride
Terry Meier

Cancer came like an ocean wave. I was floating in the ocean, me and my lump, the gentle waves cooling and rocking my body, supporting me, allowing me to be absorbed in my world. The sequence of a wave swelling up and crashing on the shore quieted me. Then a huge, strong wave with ferocious energy came rolling in. A calm sea…then this reckless wave came hurtling into my world just as my lump did.

It moved me quickly, tossing my mind and body upside-down to the sandy bottom. My vision was cloudy and salty pretzel water touched my lips and my throat, then the choking, gasping, clawing for my breath and my voice. My body didn't work and my arms were flailing up and down trying to save me, up and down and up and down again. Finally, the wave spit me out onto the shore with its last burst of energy.

My cancer had come! Now, I had to get myself up on my feet and live…only I could do that.

Once I got up, I saw people waiting impatiently and motioning to me. I slowly walked toward them; they surrounded me and gently pushed me up the beach away from the water. They spoke of biopsies, MRIs, CT scans, chemotherapy, radiation, and surgery. My brain tried to absorb their words, any words. They moved aside and there sat a shiny red wagon.

In that moment, I was a young child again. They urged me to get in with a little boy who sat behind me. Who was he? My dad, my sons, my husband, my brother? Before I had a minute to think, someone picked up the long black wagon handle. They pulled us quicker and quicker until we smashed through a white paper-thin wall. My cancer journey was on its way.

The Ride Begins

There were doctors and nurses giving me diagnoses, opinions, instructions, prescriptions, and, along with family and friends, kindness, encouragement, and support. They worked with an urgency that barely gave me a chance to catch my breath. I learned it was all about moving me through the process, along my journey. I was good at following their instructions. I showed up for my appointments, tests, treatments, and surgeries. They led; I followed!

My two thoughts were:

1) Get up and say "Good morning" and "Have a great day" to my sons, Chris and Kevin, before they went to school. If I felt sick, I could rest once they had gone for the day.

2) Go to your appointments; get your treatments and surgery. You need to do it. Get over this.

I showed up to appointments with anxiety, frustration, fear (which I wasn't even aware of), questions, angst, scars, make-up, with hair, and without hair —they took me any way I came. I didn't want any connection to the people at that 'place', the one that could save my life and make me well. Hiding in a corner was a terrific idea to me, but I kept going back. I didn't speak to anyone in the waiting rooms except my husband and the staff, if necessary.

After a few appointments my spirit and heart slowly opened. I began to smile when I saw them, particularly the nurses. The social part of me that enjoyed people and hearing their life stories surfaced; this place and the people became familiar and comfortable.

Now What?

In time, which felt like years, my hair was growing back and I was done! Treatments, surgery, radiation, complications, more surgery, medication, and then my doctor said I was 'healed'…now what??? Appointments, blood work, check-ups every three months, and CT scans once a year are the norm. I manage the anticipation of these appointments by trying to forget about them until the day comes—sometimes it works.

There were many serendipitous gifts—I met many kind, caring, and loving people. I found spiritual and inner healing through meditative and art workshops and learned it's elusive yet necessary to move forward. I was offered the privilege to form a cancer support group with several other women and an endearing holistic nurse. This nurse has peace and joy flickering about her and a 'get down to business' manner as she strives to teach me about myself and my purpose on my journey.

I am here picking up the pieces of my scattered mind and body from my ocean-blown, wagon-ride journey. This part has been the hardest. Along the way, I heard myself say, "My body was poisoned from chemo, cut and scarred from surgery, and burned from radiation, of course I'm different." The journey has not ended. I want to wake up every day, appreciate my life, feel energized and excited to be a vital part of my sons' lives, celebrate life with my family and friends, make time to play with my dog and plant my garden, laugh, smile, and know God's grace and goodness. But I don't…

Riding and Thriving

Sometimes I catch myself relishing in moments of my life and finding positive energy and love within difficult and challenging times. Deep inside me, down in my very soul, I have the awareness and words for these desires only as a result of cancer, from surviving cancer, and thriving from cancer. My inner voice presents itself in different ways, and I can hear it urging me to listen and react. I can't let myself get too low or lost. I will listen and follow slowly. The journey has not ended. The faces of the people that surround me did not change, but I am changed forever.

Meant to Be
Maureen Glennon Clayton

I have always believed that "everything happens for a reason". I was living my beautiful life and all of a sudden I was diagnosed with breast cancer? How on earth could there be reasoning behind that? Well, there was. There is. Many reasons indeed.

I remember being in my new apartment and just being happy. Two weeks prior, my family helped me move into my own space. After many years with roommates, I finally decided to get a place of my own. My apartment was so perfect for me. It was small, but big enough. I decorated it the way I wanted. I smiled every time I came home during those two weeks. Then, my life changed.

I remember getting out of the shower and going into my bedroom. I glanced in the mirror and, as I passed it, I saw something on my breast. I looked closer, thinking maybe it was just a shadow. Then, I felt it. It was an indentation. Being a dancer, I know my body, and this indentation was something different. In that moment, my life changed forever. I went full-force into action! I went to my gynecologist and she agreed it looked suspicious. She sent me for a mammogram and I made sure that my mom came with me. Yes, I was forty-one, but no matter how old you are, you always need your mom.

I knew the answer as soon as the technician excused herself from the room saying she needed additional views. I cannot believe this; I may have breast cancer. I know it; I feel it. Dammit! The technician returned and told me that a doctor was going to come in to see me. I asked that they get my mom. Dammit!

That was the next moment, the moment that I knew there would be more tests, more anxiety and much more worry. I remember being in the waiting room, feeling very vulnerable in my pink robe. They try to make that waiting room peaceful, but peace was the last thing on my mind. My mom tried to hug me and I pulled away from her. I am devastated that I did that. She wanted to comfort her baby, her first child of four, and I did not allow it.

There was another woman waiting in a pink gown, and I just couldn't break down at that moment. I just could not do that. She was where I was just a couple of minutes ago, in that world of "what if". I hate that world—but then again do I? So, "what if" I have breast cancer? I will get through it. I am a strong woman. I have a wonderful family and am blessed with many friends. I will get through this cancer adventure with open arms! I feel horrible that those arms were not open to my mom in that waiting room. When we were driving back to her house I asked my mom so...I have breast cancer? She said yes. We both cried silently.

I was diagnosed on November 13, 2009 and had a double mastectomy with breast reconstruction on December 21, 2009. The best Christmas gift was to hear that I was cancer free and could be home for Christmas. My breast reconstruction was a TRAM flap, transverse rectus abdominis myocutaneous flap. They used the muscle in my lower abdomen between my waist and my pubic bone to create breast mounds. Knowing I was a dancer, my plastic surgeon said that my dancing would probably never be the same. I responded that I'm over forty, and my dancing already isn't the same as it was so long ago!

So, my beat-up dancer body was discharged on

Christmas Eve and I was able to be with my family for the holiday. Propped up in a chair with drains, bandages, and some major painkillers, I was able to be present for all the festivities. I may not remember much, but I am sure glad I was there. I am here. I am a survivor.

Cancer has never gotten in my way in regards to things that I want to accomplish. Yes, the doctor's appointments, surgery, post-surgery appointments, and chemotherapy were a lot. But my life kept going. Both before and after surgery I kept working with my dance company, Moetion Dance Theater.

When I was first diagnosed, we were in rehearsals for a new dance piece. I was asked to create a piece about domestic abuse, and I gave my dancers some artistic instruction. We worked with gesture, a simple movement to express something. Once we all started working I began to cry. Expression through movement is so powerful. My personal feelings could not help but to show through during this rehearsal. The company and I all had a moment when I talked about how this new work is not just about domestic abuse; it is about coping with anything that life may bring. Many tears were shed during that rehearsal, and our new piece, *Cope*, was born.

The power of movement and touch is extremely healing to me. This was another moment of my cancer adventure that would make an impact on my life and the lives of others. *Movement Heals* is my workshop that I originally created for WINGS, inspired from that beautiful rehearsal. It has been one of the most amazing experiences of my life. To be able to share your feelings through movement and to express those feelings to others who have been though similar situations is a blessing.

Everyone can dance, and everyone has their own story. We use our experiences in life to guide us and make us stronger. I've always said there are pathways in life that are curvy and there are some bumps, but it is the pathway that was meant for us--to help us grow into who we are "meant to be".

As my life continued my "everything happens for a reason" phrase turned into "meant to be". It began with me being invited to an Arts & Wellness Summit—health professionals and artists coming together in the interest of well-being. I attended the conference alone and as I got out of my car I happened to see two women I worked with in the past as a guest choreographer for their organization. I called to them; they turned around and then continued to walk. I called again, same thing. I finally said, "guys, it's Moe" and they stopped. I could not understand how they didn't realize it was me, and then it dawned on me: my hair was just growing back. It never even occurred to me that someone might not recognize me, because *I am me*!

At the summit we chatted and the one woman was telling me how she met a wonderful man and was in love. I have no fear, not after what I've been through, so I asked her if she had anyone for me. She said I do, and his name is Angus. Well, that was hysterical to me because our family's dog's name was Angus! Very funny to my family too; my siblings still make comparison jokes, and my mom wanted to make sure that my Angus knew how much we all loved the other Angus. I told my colleague to give him my contact information, and after a week of not hearing anything I contacted her. I suggested that she tell him what a cool chick I was and that he should contact me. A day later he did just that, with the opening line of "I hear that you are a cool chick". Well, after about a week of emails and a couple of phone conversations I had my blind date with this man from Tennessee, Angus.

We met in a park. We walked around the town. We had dinner. And then there was that kiss. Angus would later write this to me in an email, "Yes, it was that kind of jump-start kiss…they paused in front of the restaurant, with a half turn their eyes locked. Her smile, warm and inviting. Their lips met and they both knew something had started. There can only ever be one first kiss." I remember calling my best friend on my way home to tell her what an amazing night I had on my blind date. My eyes were now open to more possibilities, and some of the bumps seemed smaller along my pathway. The next week Angus went to Tennessee for a week and then I left to teach abroad for three weeks.

We fell in love via email. It was amazing and so romantic. When I got back, we were constantly together between his apartment and mine. I met his children and we hit it off from day one. It truly does amaze me how much had happened to me in those six months after being diagnosed. That first month was one of the worst of my life and five months later was one of the best of my life. I was meant to be at that summit and was open to ask if there might be a man for me out there—and there was, and he is still here.

A bit over a year after we met we got engaged, and a year after that we got married! I was lucky enough at that time to be an advocate for Susan G. Komen for the Cure in North Jersey, getting together a team to walk a 5K to raise money and awareness. The executive director of the organization nominated me, as a breast cancer survivor, to receive a free wedding dress and up to six bridesmaid dresses. That very generous offer was yet another gift I received along this cancer journey.

Angus and I had a beautiful wedding at a museum, beginning with a very personal and touching ceremony into a wonderful reception, flash mob included! I secretly sent my flash mob tutorial to all of my family and friends and we surprised my husband and many guests with a fun-filled spontaneous dance. Spontaneity is important in life. It is an impulsive reflex. We cannot be overwhelmed with the "what if's" in life, instead we should embrace them.

Angus and I have now been married for over three years. We were recently in the process of trying to buy a house. Just like how I always had roommates and was finally excited to be on my own, Angus and I rented a couple different places before we finally decided that we needed our own place, a place to call home. Well, one drama fell into another drama with bids accepted and rejected and inspections passing and failing. It was truly a roller coaster ride. Then, we found it.

An adorable 1957 Ranch with one owner. It had the hard wood floors we always wanted and that contemporary feel that we both loved. We got a mortgage, put in a bid, and the roller coaster ride continued. It was so draining but we kept telling one another if it was meant to be we need to stick with it. After a couple of months we finally started to smooth out our ride and our new adventure began.

Our 1957 Ranch was originally owned by a couple named Mo & Gus. Well, there it was. There it is. "Meant to be" indeed...

Triple Negative
Randi E. Jeddis

December 9, 2009 was the first time I realized I could die. My mother-in-law lay in her bed at the extended care facility that had been her home for the better part of the last two years. It was a second stroke, the complications of which took her life a few days later. None of this was a surprise, as her health had been deteriorating since the previous summer.

Why did I run out of the nursing home screaming and crying? All of a sudden I grew afraid of the scene I was making in the parking lot. I stopped for a moment and looked around. Not a single solitary person seemed to care, nor did they even acknowledge what was happening right in front of them. " Randi," someone called. As the scene in my mind faded away, I realized I had only left the room in an ethereal, not physical, way. Now I really needed some space and air!

As I walked down the corridor to the elevator, all I saw were people waiting to die. Prior to my cancer diagnosis, that was not at all how I saw these very same people. I walked with a heavy heart to that same parking lot I had in my mind's eye just moments ago.

The tears and fear were very real and palpable this time. Not until that day, despite cycling through a variety of difficult thoughts and feelings, did fear of dying enter my view of the picture. Then...*IT* became the only perspective that all thoughts got filtered through. "Would I see my boys settle, get married, and have families?"

"Would there be a marital replacement for me?" "What would my legacy be?" "Did my life mean anything?" And the ever-famous, "What happens after we die?" "Nothing…? Something…?" Truth is, nobody knows 100 percent for sure.

Everyone that 1 loved was above the age of 4 and capable of remembering me on their own with the exception of one, who was only 1 ½. His memories would be comprised of stories told to him about who *I WAS.* That would be true for future grandchildren as well.

SUCKS!!! Anyone who knows me knows how much I adore kids. Prior to breast cancer one of the ways to bring me to my knees was to see adults use kids as weapons to try to settle "scores" and keep family secrets.

Cancer was equally formidable and equally able to take from me. It just wasn't personal.

September 2009

I went for my annual mammogram, and shortly after the test my doctor of about 15 years came in the exam room and said, "Randi, did you know you have a lump in your breast?" "Yes," I said. She asked me how long I had known about it, and without missing a beat I looked at my watch and said "about 3 seconds." I am nothing if not funny, and yes, I am the same girl who wore Monty Python "it's just a flesh wound" pajama pants to surgery two weeks later.

Forty-five minutes and one unscheduled biopsy later, I walked out of the office knowing I had cancer. I would have to wait twenty-four hours for the histology report, a.k.a. the next diagnostic step in figuring out just how bad *"IT"* was. Twenty-six hours later the phone rang. "Triple negative", "rare", and "aggressive" were the words that came across the telephone line connecting my ear to my doctor's mouth. I was forty-five years old.

I took a leave of absence from my private practice and became a full-time cancer-fighting employee. I knew chemotherapy, steroids, radiation, surgery and ancillary drugs were contraindicated with being a good psychotherapist for my clients. I feared the joke my kids used to make would come true if I remained at work through treatment. "My mom's a psychotherapist...yup, emphasis on the psycho."

In all seriousness, there were two very important reasons why we as a couple decided working was out until I was finished with treatment and rested. The first was that I was in for the fight of my life; triple negative breast cancer was going to be a formidable opponent and I was going to need all the energy I had to kill it. Second, working long hours with a total daily commute of two hours would water down the fight. Surgery; four rounds of Adriamycin, Cytoxan, and steroids; twelve rounds of Taxol; and thirty-five rounds of radiation would likely kill my skills as a therapist during that time period.

It was the psychologically toughest career decision I'd ever made. There was no course in grad school that covered "What To Do With Your Practice When You Get Cancer". Equally absent from my training was the chapter on how to tell clients, "I have cancer and I'm not sure when or *if* I'd be back." REALLY? I mean REALLY?

The therapeutic relationship between client and therapist is unique, and one in which the therapist is supposed to help clients resolve issues such as abandonment, not create them for fuck's sake. I had ten working days to shut it all down prior to surgery and treatment. Session after session for those ten days I said good-bye over and over again. It was the right thing to do, but it was excruciating as hell. I said my last good-bye and work was done. I turned the lights off, closed and locked the door, and promptly lost my identity for the next eighteen months.

October 8th, 2009

Surgery went well. The biopsy results would be in the next day. The eagerly awaited phone call finally came a little before noon. "Stage 1, Grade 3, ER negative, PR negative, Her2/neu or "triple negative" which is its short name. Triple negative is a rare and aggressive form of cancer, but the added piece of information surgery yielded was, "Stage 1." The tumor, despite its size, had not spread to the lymph nodes. Catching it so early was a huge prognostic plus for me.

After surgery, all I wanted was a top-notch oncologist and the prescribed treatment. I was interested in neither meeting people nor attending any cancer programs at the hospital. I was going to "do" cancer on my terms and get it behind me ASAP. Cancer was to be nothing more than a small sound byte in my life. HAH! Joke was on me!

November 29th, 2009

This is the first chemotherapy session and the beginning of "My Mondays with Michaelson." *Dr.* Michaelson, that is. In February 2010, after getting very ill with shingles, cellulitis, and MRSA, it became clear to me that my belief about needing only a good doc and treatment from the hospital couldn't have been more wrong. I called the hospital and got the name and number of the art therapist who visited me during my first chemo session. I had been pleasant during her visit weeks ago, but I threw her information away as soon as they unplugged me from the almighty IV bag that day. What the fuck was I going to do in art therapy? Instantly I had a thought: This is the beginning of my basket weaving

career! NO THANK YOU AND I RESPECTFULLY
DECLINE.
After a point, "basket weaving" seemed to have some
allure. OK. I ACCEPT. Shortly thereafter I met Lynn, and
as soon as I walked into her office I realized it was like no
other I had ever seen. Her office was a Zen Oasis in the
middle of the busy outpatient infusion center. Rena and I
met in the hospital cafeteria one day, me playing the role
of the obvious bald, bandana wearing cancer girl. I had no
idea she was a fellow cancer girl until we spoke a bit a
more that day. Shortly thereafter I met Flo, Carol B., and
Terry in groups I attended. I met the rest of the gang,
Diane, Holly, Joni, Mo and Sabina in May 2010 at a Reiki
workshop led by Lynn.

August 2010

WINGS was officially born at a local IHOP. I had
finished my last radiation treatment earlier that day. When
I walked in everyone was there and waiting. Uh, why?
Because I was waiting at the wrong IHOP 30 minutes
away. I was frazzled both by being late as well as having
had a run-in with one of my docs. When I got to the table
the magic of WINGS began for me. Each and every
woman at that table celebrated my last treatment with
happiness and clapping, and they understood my beef
with the doc. I am the usual caretaker in my life, not the
taker of care. It was wonderful yet slightly uncomfortable.

Over the last five years my WINGS sisters, as we so
affectionately call ourselves, have become close in a very
new way. This in no way mitigates the love and support I
received from some of my family and friends. I was so
fortunate to have a loving spouse by my side, and a family
to fight for. I'm simply saying WINGS has added a new
dimension of healing to my life. A dimension I could not

have imagined when I initially prepared to do the cancer trip without the assistance of anyone new in my life.

While this may sound a bit overstated, I promise you it is not. Not one of us would question being there for the other. Do we have our differing ways, views, opinions and passions? Of course we do! We're women, for God's sake! The difference with WINGS is that it is not divisive. One of the most amazing things is how each of us really cares for and respects the others. The things we might not have accepted in ourselves and each other prior to cancer are workable or become non-issues. I have come to believe it is easier to both be fallible and accept the fallibilities of others after cancer. It seems to me that cancer levels one's ego and the social playing field.

July 21st, 2015 5:07 pm

You may think the above date is reflective of some cancer milestone, anniversary or some other cancer related number time line date. While some people think it's nuts, once you have become a cancer patient numbers matter in all different kinds of ways. So, that being said, July 21, 2015…what's that? Have you ever heard "when someone dies, it's easier to remember not those that showed up, but rather those that didn't"? July 21, 2015, was the day I was able to fully integrate the pain of the aforementioned truth as it applied to cancer and me. Until recently, I rationalized why some important family and friends didn't show up, but remained grateful to those that did. The people list in the book of my life took some unexpected hits. Yes, they are hits; however, those have cleared room for some amazing additions.

Relationships that were strong remain strong, relationships that were broken remain broken, relationships that were precarious have been relinquished to their proper place, and relationships that were emerging have gotten stronger. Lastly and most importantly, acquaintances disguised as intimate and caring relationships are properly placed back in the acquaintance column. All human beings deal with crisis differently, and this applies equally to cancer. Life is busy, the world spins, and there is so much life still to live. There is no more time to focus on the pain. I choose to focus on those who did and still do show up.

I now have sisters with whom unconditional love is the rule, not the exception. Water really can be stronger than blood. We are "sisters from different misters" and "sisters from other mothers". No blood…but an amazing amount of water.

I AM OH SO GOOD WITH THAT!!!!

THE ROOT CHAKRA

"True stability results when presumed order and disorder are balanced." ~ *Tom Robbins*

The first chakra is an earth-red color and is located at the base of the spine. We feel grounded by this chakra. Since it is closest to the earth, we also feel rooted to Mother Earth and our family of origin. It is our connection to traditional family beliefs that support the formation of identity and a sense of belonging. It is the beginning of safety and security in our lives.

When our root chakra is open, it not only gives us a feeling of safety, but it also generates a sense of security and peace to those around us. It aligns us with universal energy, which is spiritual energy, and it allows our wishes to become reality by removing obstacles that are standing in our way.

Angels and Demons
Rena Cooper

She knew what it felt like to live with demons at an early age. An unhappy childhood rooted her in a place she didn't want to be. Not feeling safe with a loved one created a place in her heart where demons could thrive. They brought fear with them. Fear of the dark, ghosts, and lightning. Her worst fear was of being abandoned, and separation anxiety controlled her earliest years.

Her angels didn't show up until much later in her life, just in time to keep the switch from being thrown. Was she worthy enough to escape the cancer demons that had plagued her family? The more she feared the cancer, the more she fought its existence. The more she fought, the more afraid she became. The demons had taken over her soul. They were mottled through her heart like fat through a juicy steak. Only now they meant to kill her.

She prayed for healing and sought out any logical treatment that might help…some did, most didn't. Yet ever so slowly, her angels began to arrive. They came in the form of a supportive, loving husband and a few close friends. She felt her connection to God through the precious creatures that warmed her home. They brought her a joy that filled the missing pieces of her fractured heart.

She needed those angels now more than ever. They kept the demons cordoned off in her body like a military squad. After almost 6 years of remission, the angels have allowed the demons to escape their captors for yet another try at erasing her. Maybe she wasn't important or worthy enough. Perhaps the angels no longer felt as needed. It looked as if everything was under control, so they seemed to be drifting away—perhaps to find another person circling the drain?

Now her heart is searching for the right balance to keep the demons from tipping the scales in their favor. She agonizes over how to make her angels stay. She prays to her angels every day. Her prayer is always the same.

"Please don't leave me."

She Is From
Holly Whitmore Denton

She is from…

The mother and father who loved each other so…
Who then loved her too.
To California and back again.
California, fornia, fornia…

She is from…

A lovely town and summered at the shore, where she was in the bubbles show every year and sang with her brother and sister.

Her brother—such an amazing musician. He played his guitar every night while they cleaned up the kitchen and really believed he was helping. Well, he *was* helping, but not exactly helping clean up.

Her sister who could play the flute and had a beautiful voice too, but did back flips through the living room to keep up with her siblings.

She is from the mother who has M.S. The mother who endured, struggled and still was able to give as her body failed—as she became more like the child than the mother—but still was.

She is from the father who started out so strong but was beaten down by the cruel disease that lassoed his beautiful wife.

She is from the northeast but was schooled in the south and learned to say, "Bless her heart," in order to get away with a bit of gossip.

She is from Brooklyn and NYC where she lived and worked, and knew every hot restaurant and where everyone should go...

She is from the suburbs but said, "Absolutely not!" to that minivan, until she realized she could control all the windows with one button—well, ok, a minivan.

She is from…

Hawaii where she had her honeymoon with that adorable and funny guy who has ten great siblings and beautiful parents.

She is from Verona, with three magnificent boys who wore pink shirts to school when she was diagnosed.

She is from Breast Cancer…

But not always.

CLOSING THOUGHTS

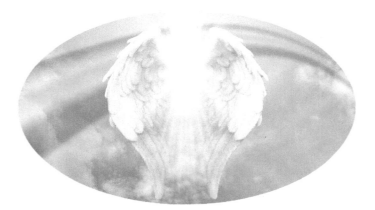

My Spirituality
Lynn Ferrer

*"The idea is to write it so that people hear it and it
slides through the brain and goes straight to the heart."*
~ Maya Angelou

What do Maya Angelou's beautiful words mean to me?
They speak to my spirituality and who I really am! Have I
explored that subject enough, or am I still just scratching
the surface? I truly believe the question needs to be asked
on a daily basis. Each day traveling a little deeper and
uncovering more of our precious gems. For me, it is a
lifelong journey and an important part of my being.

I began questioning spirituality at an early age and
have continued throughout my life. To answer this
question, using only my brainpower is never enough. I
must bring it into my Heart and allow these gifts to help
shape my responses and actions. Now, is it enough? What
about my soul and spirit? These, too, need to play a
prominent role in my decision-making and goals.

I now need to answer the second question: what do I
want? What do I truly want from this world? At the age of
78, am I satisfied with my life? Are the demons prodding
me while the Angels patiently sit on my shoulders
reminding me that they are here to stay? My daily dose of
gratitude keeps me balanced so that I can listen to the
whispers of my heart and soul.

Now, where do I go from here? How do I serve? There
are so many ways, both big and small. By following my
Sacred Contract, which was tucked right under my arm
when I came into this world, I stay on my path. The
journey is not always easy, and there are many challenges
to face, but as Mother Teresa states, "I know God won't

give me anything I can't handle. I just wish He didn't trust me so much."

Namaste!

My Journey
Sister Carol A. Jaruszewski R.S.M.

"You'll never walk alone." These words from a song can be so assuring when experienced by someone in their mind, body, and spirit. As a spiritual seeker, I have been a religious woman for fifty years as a Sister of Mercy. Unique to my community is that we take a fourth vow of service: service to the poor, sick, and uneducated. One of the prayers our foundress would pray has these words, which have become my prayer as well: "My God, I am yours for time and eternity."

I have been blessed with a childhood in which I experienced faith and the belief that I was loved and beautiful, especially through my grandmother, Anna. She became a messenger of the Divine. To have this deep awareness within is a spiritual gift, one that assures a person that nothing can separate her from love. In my tradition, God is love.

Spirit is essential for the journey of life. It needs to be nourished, and we are always invited to reflect and become aware of Spirit's presence in our daily life, especially in our relationships with all of creation.

How do you nurture your spirit? Meditation, nature, reading, worship, music, art? We are invited to seek the spiritual.

"You are God's work of art." These words from a song encourage us to study, learn, and be open to the new ways we are co-creating with our God. I have been able to walk with others, encouraging them to grow in mind, body and spirit. As an art teacher of K thru 12, as a director of retreats for all ages, and being invited to lead retreats for the board of WINGS has been a privilege and delight. Gathering at Mary's Place near the sea in Ocean Grove, New Jersey, we extended our hospitality to women who have been diagnosed with cancer. Together with the board members of WINGS we supported each other in helping women dealing with their disease, and reaching out in service to other women to inspire, nurture, and lend strength and support to them as they walk their journeys to wellness each day.

As God's work of art we continue to be created anew. We each have a wondrous body, and choosing to care for the body is vital. As children we are guided to healthy eating and exercise. When we stop caring for the body, the stresses of life will physically manifest. Our many responsibilities and the pace of our society do not always encourage us to find ways and means to release emotions or tensions, and thus disease enters our body.

I have ovarian cancer, which has reoccurred several times in spite of chemo, radiation, scans, special trials, and more chemo over the years. I am still in treatment. As a trained spiritual director I have companioned women with cancer, sharing my gift of counseling, healing touch, aromatherapy, and art, as well as Tai Chi Chih, a form of Qi Gong.

As a woman in treatment I now know the walk in a different way and treasure the women in my life with whom I share this reality. Hoping each day is a good day of body and spirit for them, I pray to live my vow of compassionate service to the sick. I receive so much in return from them as we walk with each other and gather monthly in Verona for our WINGS support group for a healing arts experience and sharing.

How are *you* caring for *your* body? Massage, Reiki,

nutrition, tai chi, walking, exercise?

"To love another person is to see the face of God." These words from the play "Les Misérables" inspire me. I have learned and studied in school a variety of subjects, and I realize we never stop learning. I desire to be open-minded, to listen and learn from others who are teachers in my life—teachers by words and example. The mind and our thoughts have such power. It is said that "Energy follows thought." It has been vital for me to be positive, to be self-affirming. Sharing words and thoughts of hope and encouragement as I walk with others and have others walk with me has had the profound impact of miracle and mystery.

I have found that the practice of gratitude each day deepens the joy and love you experience. We can choose what we want to think and believe.

What thoughts dominate your mind? What do you choose to read, watch, and take in?

In the words of Pope Francis…"Move forward."

So if you are reading this book of sacred stories, know there are people in your life who have been sent to walk the journey with you.

You will never walk alone...

You are God's work of art.

And recognize that to love and be loved by another person is to see the face of God.

Blessings on your journey…

ABOUT WINGS
Our Mission

To provide a positive environment for women affected by cancer—before, during and after treatment—to alleviate stress and anxiety through the healing arts.

WINGS is a Women's Cancer Support group in Verona, New Jersey. Monthly programs include educational topics, guest speakers, as well as group support to help regain physical, emotional and spiritual health.

We gratefully accept donations and appreciate your support. To make a donation, please visit our website or send an email.

Website: www.wingscancersupport.com
Email: wingscancerhelp@gmail.com

WINGS BOARD MEMBERS

*"Be bold and brave in your heart
and let it lead the way."*

Holly Denton, President and Founding Member
I was diagnosed with breast cancer in October of 2008. Even before having my bi-lateral mastectomy and chemotherapy, I began to understand and feel the incredible healing power of love, support and of women sharing and listening who had had similar experiences. Being a musician, and working in music with young families, I was acutely aware of the many ways music could help in healing. But then delving into the healing arts more fully as I went deeper with all of our WINGS programs, I have learned so much more about the whole mind, body and spirit connection. Meeting holistic nurse Lynn Ferrer and the subsequent formation of WINGS Cancer Support Group has been another incredible journey that continues to bring, joy, peace and inspiration. I am a mother of three boys, wife, sister of a cancer survivor, and feel so blessed to be able to pay it forward through WINGS.

Diane Braschi, Vice President and Founding Member
I am a mother, daughter, friend and survivor. I was diagnosed with rectal cancer at the age of forty-seven and have been living cancer-free for five years. I believe that my faith, the healing arts and the support of the Women of WINGS, have been essential to my recovery and peace of mind. I want women to know that we need not be alone; the women of WINGS stand together and offer Love, Hope, Comfort and Support.

Randi Jeddis, Treasurer and Founding Member
In September 2009 at the age of 46 I was diagnosed with a rare and aggressive form of breast cancer. Today I am cancer free. Little did I know that on this journey, I would meet a group of amazing women and that together we would turn WINGS from a concept in to a program. Being both a founding member and a member of the board of directors has brought an amazing amount of joy, fulfillment, and support to me over the last five years. The woman on the Board and all the women who have attended our programs have added depth and quality to both my recovery and my life. I consider it an honor to lead the support group that we have directly after most presentations.

Rena Cooper, Secretary and Founding Member
I am a retired elementary school teacher. Six months into retirement, the proverbial rug was pulled out from under me. Stage 4 uterine cancer! Thankfully, that was not my end, but rather the beginning of a new perspective on life. As a founding member of WINGS, I've had the satisfaction of seeing the strength, energy and caring that our support group has provided to women on their cancer journey. WINGS has been my life raft; helping me to cope with my situation and to see the positive possibilities. The camaraderie I feel meeting with women sharing my experience is priceless. During the monthly meetings, we learn how to better help ourselves through the healing arts. We also get to share our good news and concerns when we need to. Don't just settle for being a cancer survivor, learn how to be a cancer thriver. I've been enjoying my life for the past 6 years and plan to continue.

Terry Meier, Founding Member
I am grateful to be a mother and wife, sister, friend and dog lover. I believe Hope is the theme throughout my life, particularly in my breast cancer journey. Volunteer work has become my focus in both schools and in the community. It is a privilege to serve as a member of WINGS.

Joni Jasterzbski, Founding Member
I am a mother of two daughters, a wife of 28 years, an elementary school art teacher for 30 years and a stage 3 breast cancer survivor/thriver. I was very scared when diagnosed and throughout all the treatments and surgery, but surviving cancer has given me a new outlook and appreciation for life and for all the positive that has come out of this experience. I have witnessed incredible acts of kindness and have met so many beautiful people on this journey. I am involved with an organization called Hearts of Hopeand have created and distributed over 5000 painted ceramic hearts to local hospitals over the last six years. I am lucky to be on the board of WINGS with amazing women, where we continue to pay forward love, kindness and understanding. I try to find the good that I can do and live life to the fullest every day.

Maureen Glennon Clayton, Founding Member
Being diagnosed with breast cancer in November 2009 was one of the worst events in my life but ended up being one of the most rewarding. I am a dancer, choreographer and dance educator. Dance is my life and when diagnosed I was in rehearsals with my dance company, Moe-tion dance theater, and also working at my full-time job, as a dance instructor, at a gifted and talented high school dance program. The support and love I received from my family, friends, colleagues and students helped me push

through obstacles. Through laughter and tears, my company and I collaborated on a new dance piece. Being able to express myself through movement was, and is so healing. I appreciate every single moment of my "cancer adventure". I believe that everything happens for a reason. I was introduced to these beautiful women through our shared holistic nurse Lynn. Together, WINGS was born. I am grateful for every day that was and look forward to every day to come.

Lynn Ferrer, RN, MA, HNB-BC - Founding Member
I am Lynn Ferrer, a Holistic Nurse Practitioner, working in the outpatient cancer program at Saint Barnabas Medical Center, who is gratefully living her "Sacred Contract." I am passionate about my work and I love my patients dearly. I am honored to be a Founding Member of the WINGS Cancer Support Group for Women, and I feel truly blessed to be able to share my life with these courageous ladies.

HONORARIUM

Florence Schwartz-Siderman
June 29th 1945-May 22nd 2012

This book serves as a loving memory to Flo Siderman. Flo was a loving wife, mother, grandmother, friend and one of the original and founding board members of WINGS. Flo was passionate about WINGS and our mission. The last year of Flo's life was very difficult as she had been re-diagnosed with Leukemia and subsequently had a bone marrow transplant that failed. Unfortunately Flo never regained her physical health prior to her death in May of 2012.

Though the treatments and cancer left her physically weakened, her spirit, love of life and hope for remission remained until the end. Her love for her sons, husband

and granddaughter, Lyla were so palpable whenever she spoke of them. Her twin grandchildren born after her death would have simply put her over the moon.

There are so many wonderful stories we could share about Flo, but the following seems most appropriate. One particular night a few months after Flo's transplant the weather was quite harsh. It was freezing cold and despite knowing Flo wanted to attend our monthly meeting, we all had our doubts. We all underestimated Flo, because shortly after our speculations stopped, there she was! She was impeccably dressed, which was normal for her—and only she could make a hospital mask and gloves look chic. That was the last meeting she was able to attend.

Through the last three years our memories, moments and stories of Flo have been somewhat of a comfort. If Flo were with us today, there is no doubt that you would get to know her intimately through what she would have shared in this book.

Life is a Gift
Embrace every moment
and Cherish This
Gift !

Flo Silerman

CPSIA information can be obtained at www.ICGtesting.com
Printed in the USA
BVOW11s1942250116

433976BV00008B/10/P